BUTCHER'S TREE

Butcher's Tree

by Feng Sun Chen

Black Ocean
Boston · New York · Chicago

Black Ocean
P.O. Box 52030
Boston, MA 02205
blackocean.org

Cover illustration by Josh Wallis
Book design by Janaka Stucky

ISBN 978-0-9844752-4-7

Library of Congress Cataloging-in-Publication Data

Chen, Feng Sun, 1987-
Butcher's tree / Feng Sun Chen.
    p. cm.
Poetry.
ISBN 978-0-9844752-4-7
I. Title.
PS3603.H4475
811'.6--dc22

                    2011049387

Printed in Canada
FIRST EDITION

CONTENTS

[Milk Vein]

[Wolf Teeth]

[Grendel is a Woman]

ACKNOWLEDGMENTS

I would like to thank the wonderful Black Oceanographers for helping me realize this book, and for putting up with my amorphousness. I am also grateful to my loved ones, my teachers, guides, and my cat for their support and their sublime strangeness.

Some poems have appeared in slightly altered form in the following journals: *Bathhouse*, *Blood Lotus*, *Conduit*, *Diagram*, *La Fovea*, *La Petit Zine*, *New Delta Review*, *nthposition*, *Pop Serial*, *Moon Milk Review*, *Radioactive Moat*, *So and So*, *Word Riot*, *Strange Machine*, *Super Arrow*, *Weave*, and *White Whale Review*.

Thanks also to: Federico del Sagrado Corazón de Jesús García Lorca (invoked in Grendel's poem), Robert Frost (a reference in "Fountain of Youth"), Sylvia Plath (various quotes in "Moontube"), Franz Kafka's "The Silence of the Sirens" is referenced and quoted in the Grendel poem (mostly in section 6, but echoes throughout), and some words were taken from *The Holy Bible*.

[MILK VEIN]

BY THE DARK

Two travelers boil in it.
Curtains of dry rock drink the glue
of their sweat.

Maybe they have
a train to catch
or the field of soft stone is a field of milk teeth

they cannot sleep as dreams snag in the esophagus
tear through twin hearted flesh
through bones made of shale.

One can see the other's rage.
His rage is small but dense. It catches the wet light
by its webbed gravity.

He looks up at the dark
socketed between a ring of mountains.

Rage grows smaller and denser
with each point of old light.

That there should be so much walking
and so much distance
even burnt comets must pass.

That his shame should come so far.
That none of this could release him.

The skin on his forehead is pulpy.

He could go back to the woods.

He could go back to the sea if he closed his eyes.

No going anywhere.
His two hearts are growing teeth.

FOURTH OF JULY

Sometime, said the paper queen, you will cease to be loved.
Maybe you will be lucky
and a kind witch will tell you why. It's probably your personality,
for example. You will not understand your pain,
which is shaped like a windmill and moves
by the tug of a horrible moon
but you may learn to live with it, or forget it
for longer and longer stretches.
In this case, the story must rest
on my profound endurance.
What a long time I have gone on! Even after the baby dropped
and happiness has proven itself to parts of the world
like glow on a map of electric consumption,
a country of darkness
wrung with glitter. I want to kill
you, with my glittering heart. I can never stop
until I do. But I am small.
Maybe, said the magic vole, you are too small.
Maybe, said the naked mole, you will have to give up, or somehow
eat it up from the inside.
There are other things to think about, said the princess
in a dress made of leaves, such as art. Where is your warm gun?
Let freedom sprout. Show me how you love.
Spangled one, how precarious and plump you look
perched on a white fence. Happiness, said the paper
beggar, who is really a god,
comes from within. Oh, how he hobbles! Look on, look on.
He is richer than you. There are forces

much larger at work here,
humming about like godmothers.
I am small, I am small. Here comes the parade! All that beauty!
I want to die! I want to die!
I want to die!

GEOLOGY

I would never eat a whale
but I love the petrified tear of a precarious boy.

The edge of life
sits on a ruined nucleus.

Lattice of gone mother.
Pulp of split sister.

Suddenly earth sings of packed nights.
When the blood in the brain coagulates

to form tiny atria.
When the soul steps from the body

and watches the body
and the body is flayed.

Mantles of blood glide over the pebble of
soldiered joy

when the child in the child or the child in the grown body
is cast under the surface.

This is where the pith is refined.
Take away the human.

Calling drips
through the cored body.

PROMETHEUS

Fire was not worth it
but I won't take it back.

The birds were not worth it. The trees were not.
Nor the red boil of sky. Nor the froth of the sea.

Not even Paris.

It was only a little trick.
A little slant of the eye.

Don't go near the women, father said
until you've been good and hurt, and the girl too.

I suppose pain is fancy like that.

Though it began like that. The gods are very pretty.
But have you ever seen
a girlboy lashed with wings? It was their
walking carelessly under a skyhole or two
suddenly struck by golden rays on the shoulder blades.

They are so appreciative
of anything we give them. They speak in tongues!

I wasn't trying to impress anyone. The Olympians
can go suck on the clouds.

What can one do? I could not die
for the suffocating awakeness; the gods are like sharks
and do not truly sleep. We sleep as androids do. In pretense.

Not even love. Though it came close.

You'll never guess.

It was the man pulling his teeth out in the woods
for his dead wife. The inverse song.
What is as uniquely satisfying? To think that I should never
satisfy this eternal itch!

My livers could fill whole oceans, several planets worth.
Meaningless livers. Endless livers.

I can't say it. The word is ripped from me daily.
I have become a huge liver. A liver of it.

EITHER

Flung curtain shift
of bluescreen retina—
is it not such

outward pleasure that makes
the inner cells grow big;
Either a screaming
that pulls with it
a document of earliness

when god's many hands
tipped with unethical electricity
scorched the earth,
either it is soundless

screaming lugged
from its white grub's slumber
shout that wraps itself around

marrow of hunger
either it is
or it is not

MOONTUBE

"Does not my heat astound you. And my light"

I will take the plastic flippers off your feet and put my lips to your feet.
This is not to kiss your skin
or to touch deeper organ.

I will put my mouth to your mouth. It doesn't have to be a mouth.
Your nose is fine. An ear. Maybe my ear to your mouth.

Your hollowness to meet my hollowness.
Your cave to link to mine
and then the voicebox becomes obsolete.

Don't want to eat you. Don't want to touch you. Don't want to enter you.

I will show you the common satellite.
We can go grocery shopping or watch the sunset.
Then I want to put my mouth over your mouth.

One stab of outside through our body. Out throughout.
I know you are very beautiful.

No time machine or capsule could make you more beautiful.
But that is an aside.

"Pure? What does it mean? / The tongues of hell"

The wind will blow through us, one string.

Our skins fuse like early cells to become one sheet.

I will sing to you and to me, larynx twinned.
No one will hear. We will be the only ones, the one canal,
the one curled snail and hammer to the brain.

Real ecstasy is stasis.
I will keep my mouth on your mouth.
Our blood will mix, grape on grape, crushed seed.

"Your body / hurts me as the world hurts god"

Hurt sits in the chest.
Purity strips the meat from inside.

TROPE

Someone kneads the bones to a pulp.
Fear suckles on black paws.
I bang the containers in the kitchen, ceramic cymbals,
fat wooden ladles rough with fissures.

Blinds scale glass that does not keep the liquid fire out.
It drips cleaner-fluid thick, reverberating with the bell
of a dark place of worship.

Feel something recede into a damp echo tunnel.
Rush to the sink. Inside the drain, blades and a few strawberry leaves.
Call into it. Spindly clock hands
make pain sounds as they fall down. Do it.

The room grows bigger, and something squirms.
My throat hurts.

I want to be alone with the ghosts.
I will humiliate them, make them flatter me, make them stand in the light
and laugh at their transparency.

Recall a face, long and horrible and lovely and vulpine.
The meat hook staggers closer to the left atrium.
It is an old scene, well played, but something's been deflated.
The sand in the bag fallen out.

Eyes drizzle across the basket of old ribbons.
Repetition does nothing to blunt a face.

Matchstick head
in its place. Knuckles in the mouth. White, red.
These are tooth-marks. They make baby birds in the hand open up.
Light passes through the skin and the small dark grasses lift up their blind eyes.

If I didn't have to take you by force from somewhere inside,
each drag would be honest for the unfading strangeness.

I do this at the dinner table. I boil it and eat a salad and duck meat
and the old light enters and I flutter like an ax and I laugh.

PLAY

Thousands share his name. Brown eyes, two out of sixteen billion.
Brown hair, ten thousand out of trillions.
Pink worm lips, pink worm tongue.

His brain is pink, I say, as is his skin, especially in the heat.
His hair expands in the humidity. In the spring, anxieties pop up in the field
of him like Birds of Paradise.

He has very long lashes, like a camel. They rhyme out like bells.
For these bells I am sent through rooms
filled to the beams with waxy meat. A hall of tongues, a corridor of knees,
hands and banquet hall of legs lids and lips and some with just the scalp.

My ears ring silver. There is no time.

The minotaur with the scalpel waves it around, sparkling.

Go ahead, he says, reconstruct him.
I see that he is the god of undoing. He can outdo even himself.

I wake up later and it is muggy outside
and I've already forgotten what it was like in the winter
when I could still see my breath
and remember how the world enters me that way.

The bells in the winter rang truer. What can I say? His name? A name? Name
of a muscle?

Can't say it. Can't kill it.

Burn up the futurist museums.
The paintings will come to life.

Rip everyone apart. Rip everything.

When I see the mosaic of red on the train track, I think of the rooms, the name.

The smell of it, the smell of the wild when the wild is gone,
forests of clear membranes, loud blood and a few edge bells.

STORY I HEARD WHILE IN BED

The first of seventy-two transformations happened without awareness.

Wukong was afraid to fall asleep because his sense half-closed like a shy fern.
He thought he would die
if he stopped thinking for one second
and sleep was like that.

He did not transform into something else. He was a kite and he was not a kite,
flying itself.

In sleep Wukong was pure,
he felt like a salmon inside a bear.

Purer than water almost.
Even in his dreams it was something else that moved
through him, the purity of foul smells,
pungent tangle from the soil.

Something elemental. Something watched himself dream.

The gut crushing brainfruit festered through the night
and he stayed up shaving turnips with a cheese grater, making cold salads.

He knew he would have to give in.

WET WINDOW

He met a girl in diving class with transparent flippers. The girl owned a camera and a mirror and brought both with her when she dived. Actually, she carried both around with her everywhere. Wukong wondered if she even kept the camera around her neck when she bathed or changed. He became fascinated with the way grammar did things to people. When she put different clothes on or took them off, she changed. It isn't supposed to say anything about her essence, but Wukong knew it did. He had a conch shell. He turned the conch and put it to her ear once, but all subsequent experiences with the conch consisted of looking at its underside, the withered yet wet mouth. When he looked at the girl with transparent flippers, he knew that if he looked at her underneath side, he would be able to hear a sound of the wind leaving, or water falling. It would be salty. It would be alive. It would contain a creature with a heart that used no arteries or veins but whose blood bathed its organs in a single cavity. He thought of doors as smacking, windows as puckering. Every opening meant access to the sea now, or the wind on the sea.

SCRIPTURES

On the hottest day of the year, bright flowers tweezed from the ground.
Whitehot pincers lowered and then closed and retreated.
The earth winced.
One of the pincers drove its beak into Wukong's chest.
His ribs were giving birth.
The petals were like the lightfish that used to swim in the waterfall back
home. They flapped in the chest.

Are we there yet.
We are not.
India is far.
The sun is near.

More and more Wukong loved darkness,
Everything that burned fire, that charred light.

The tender flesh of Xuanzang
glinted like the whites of eyes.
What is this, he wondered, wanting to make skin cry.
Is it serrated or smooth?
Maybe it is not sharp
but a dull feeling.
He wrapped it around himself and Xuanzang.
Nothing he hated
more than the sun.
How it ached and whimpered, not daring hard enough
to break through.

Light dripped from his cruel eyes.
He hoped India would hold the metallic flower of love
like the pit of a blender.
He hoped it would spin and spin.
He would jump right into the heart of it.
He hoped the heart would turn
against itself and burrow through the meat mantle.
The earth as a bead waiting to be strung.
If he ate the flesh of Xuanzang, would he be inhabited by him?
Does India have milk?
Does India love suffering?
He would never stop returning.

FOUNTAIN OF YOUTH

Someone took out a triangle of flesh from his forehead.
Inside was more sight. Pieces of broken glass reflected
their spidery faces in fragments of eight.

The girl in the transparent flippers held his arm as they lurched to the sidewalk.
His tail was beginning to bleed again. There was a pool of it on the ground
leading into the tavern. It was like a forest, the blood, deep and dark.

Don't worry, he said, I cannot die.
But the girl looked at him with unstable eyes filled with black dust.
You are mistaken, said those eyes swirling with black dust.
Wukong held on to the swung bar of life in a dance without ground. How
am I mistaken?
A name in a book is nothing, said those female eyes black with swirling dust,
You will lose.

She looked quite old fashioned in a long pleated gown of soft cream,
now rusted with blood.
Wukong laughed blood until he cried blood.
How full of blood I am, he cried.

He could see evil with those coal red eyes.
He could see she wanted to suck his blood,
lie down and whet her body on the soaked cement.

And how does a woman refuse death? Wukong asked.
The girl crouched beside him.
I am not a woman.
His eyes seemed to retreat like dark fish.

IN THE BEGINNING

One of the things they did was ferment peaches and grapes
in the hollows of their cheeks.
Each day was filtered through the wall made of movement.
The exposed king languidly sprawled
on the rock from which he sprang.
Everything came from this, he said.
Wukong camped by the waterfall
a few feet from the rock from which he sprang.
He drank the water from the wall
that separated this from that.
He'd harvested dozens of monkey hearts and they slept
quietly like potatoes in a pile by the rock.
You know what your problem is? X asked, smiling—
You're too self-involved. It's like having an imaginary friend.
The king of the primates played with a moth in his hand.
He knew that X was wrong. It was not about self.
The moth was white and furry. From its tiny feelers
music flapped. The hand folded, long fingers warped
into cochlea. Every sound reverberated through his fist.
Inside the hearing fist was wet with moth.
How could he believe in a self like a leaf
so easily crushed. There is no such thing as
time for everything, this much was clear.

HADES

One day the girl dived
to go pearl harvesting
and was never heard of again.
Perhaps the water was too thick
for her cries to reach shore.
Perhaps she is still
there, in a cave, laden
with pearls, rich with light waiting
to hatch out,
her hands cupping thousands
of pale eyeballs.

[WOLF TEETH]

EPISTLE

Words of wisdom collect in the corners of the room.

I gyrate about in a puffy suit filled with hair.

It takes me out of the circus
into the arena of history, which is full of white horses.

The knight of joy is not fickle.

Anything is permissible as long
as it is explosive.

I am the knight and I am the jester, and I descend.

What a mountain really is.

A gash the shape of you my friend
casts a nimbus through my head.

ETHICS

Nothing is as interesting
or boring to me as death,
so I take it and give it to you.

You and me, two flagella
in a sea of mucus.

Remember Sada? She was a real
Lady Lazarus.
Our bodies radiate from hers.
She is packed with energy.

Capsule from which we hang, we
two pieces of flay.
Two muscle fibers.

I want to take you
and carry your softness
around in newspaper.

You are the soup
that fills my skull.

You are criminal nonsense.

You will be hanged
because the word we're guessing at
does not exist.

Vladimir will tell you
about the excitement
swift and pretty.

Dreams are the perfect act.
Anything can be taken back.

Soft, hot roads bend
back into themselves, rings
within rings like a butcher's tree.

This is perfect.

Yesterday, I amputated
something personal and felt
like an archeologist.

There grew a new skin for it.
Joiehorroroccus in a petri dish.

Pale, small, the color
of blanched skin with a little bit
of pink and blue.
Messy and dumb
leaking outside the lines.

It felt like something from a plant,
bunched and grainy and full of seeds.

Thank you for meeting here my joy
said one horror to the other.
This is a bright habitat.

CONCERNING NOTHING

1. By finite, I mean a thing caught in time, thing that changes
    and eventually loses the original qualities that made it such.
    Starfish, one might suspect, are not finite.
    They move deceivingly through the lava of time.
    The cat on my lap is finite.
    I will watch it go through the various stages of adorability, change, fatten,
    perhaps wither, definitely die; and its body will become the worm or it
    may be cast into a blue flame and turned into dust.
    My pet rock will remain itself longer than I or the cat, but it is also finite.
    I am sad.

2. By infinite I do not mean unlimited, but a limitation incapable of change.
    What is infinite is outside of time.
    Our universe is not infinite.
    Invisible things collide and this is called energy.
    Souls are eardrums.
    They vibrate and burst.
    This noise that passes.
    We hum an infinite number of times.
    Love secretes reptile eggs into the ruptured drum nest.
    This is what we hear.

3. If knowledge hears the mind and if the mind hears the brain,
   then knowledge is not infinite.
   The egg hatches and the bundles fall out and scream diamond-mouthed.
   Something is known outside the context of brain scribble.
   The bundles have heavy holes and the holes know something.
   Don't touch it.
   Don't take it apart.
   I am afraid.

4. By hunger I mean more.
   Being contingent on objects of desire.
   The cat on my lap is always hungry.
   Cats do not possess the chemical that signals fullness.
   Desire means that the looking glass is always partly empty.
   They nap in the sun and are attracted to bright patches of carpet.
   The cat runs to the wet bundle in the grass and pounds it.
   I am not infinite.
   I am hungry.

5. An idea is a beast that emerges as the sum of specific, corresponding
   conceptual electrical pathways.
   An idea is the mass of fish darkening the blasted sky.
   Together they form a motivated sphere.
   Electricity looks white, so white it skins your knees.
   Think about the idea of eating winter, touching your winter,
   and then feel as if a winter has passed,
   and you are alone with ashamed talons and alive loneliness.
   I am lonely.

6. By mean I mean.
   When I say something concerning night, concerning the heavy, banana-ripe moon snagged in the branches when I say it is a bowl of cherry meat,
   I don't mean it. You're not average, baby, I love you.
   Somebody grabs my arms and squeezes my ribcage in terror.
   I mean it, I say.
   Like a bird bundle, the word shrieks in fury and does not point.
   Worms must somehow be unearthed.
   They must somehow fly.
   The nest continues to grow.

7. To mean is to entail is to intend.
   The idea of this is
   starfish begin to encroach on trees.
   I didn't mean monsters.
   I don't believe in what I mean.
   The talons are beaks.
   I don't mean anything I believe.
   To desire, one must believe.
   This is not strong desire.
   It is the life of dust.
   In spite of.
   I mean to believe. I miss.

CONCERNING REPETITION

I am a good person with a bad heart.

The photographer takes a picture of a thousand open refrigerators.
Because refrigerators are inhabited more than bodies are.

You are the soup that fills my skull.
You will be hanged because the world we're guessing at doesn't exist.

Roads bend back into their own meatus.
Yesterday, I amputated it.
If only I could show you.

It was the color of blanched skin with a little bit of pink and blue.
I put it in the fridge above the lettuce, next to the butter.
The photographer takes it out because it is too artificial.
What can I say?

You can tell anyone anything if it happened in a dream.

COMFORT WOMAN

We of the cave,
like dark milk newts
swim through the anti-nights.

To speak eyes is to
moth in a vacuum.

Cells punctuated
glitter nice.

An older mind
ends our sentences.

All nose, the stink is creation.
The fume of promise, the snails
in their skin water
stink of men.

Fingers trace the railroads
of combat souvenirs.

Still, just degrees
in a spectrum of innocence.

Presence by intensities
of blues and blacks
tolerance of pressure
on the back.

Hang the last word
in the body
from a tree, black.

INTER

The doctor gave me a ladle and said have some while it's still hot;
then I understood why the x-ray was horizontal.
It was foggy like shark fin soup. I drank the thickness of light
tables, the setting of a square sun.

So is this where the trouble is?
Little gumdrop fish have camped out in the forest of alveoli.
Yes, said the doctor, but you see that is not the important part.
The X is not there. X is where the treasure is.
I'm a firm believer in material value, he said,
everything meaningful is solid.

I had some more soup and left.
My friends tell me I am eating myself,
and they are right. Only a friend could be so insightful.
They surround me like trees
scattering coins of sun from their hair.

They are jealous of the new tadpoles living inside my body. It is almost spring
and the red garden is sprouting. Tangles of subways run
frenzied through the new cities. The red noise
that lives in the center ribbits, faster and slower, slower then faster.
He means to say they too want light.

My friends are radiant.
They dance until they vomit.

They are caught up
in the integrity of the body.
I think it is sweet
how the flesh curdles.

The morning increases in urgency
and the cold lemon brow of the sky stretches tight.
Soon there will be rupture.

NEON PARADE

Walk down the alley on stilts
from wanting to see far enough fast enough.

Your clown suit is soiled and your red smile smeared bigger
than your vocabulary and the rhythm of rough wood on puddled ground
has its own theory of cartography incongruous

with your horseshoe heart. It is not raining but you know it is
somewhere, maybe inside one of the buildings maybe inside

your house of bone and water and all the surfaces limpid wet
the alley path compromised by waxy spots where your stilts sink in
further each time, each time the map of your circuitry broadens

starbursts in your chest scattering evidence
that everything you ever wanted will be taken from you.
clarity is not crisp, you cry, face paint caking with particles

in the omnipotent wind in the autumn. Autumn is not crisp!
Leaves are not crisp! Now you see the half life of your
uranium nucleus compact, threatening a blank.

But you must not think about it. You step giraffely over a
family of trenchcoats and a sore foot sticking out from a porch.

Hear some distant song that is not a foghorn but
a sleeping baby and your stilts shortening, grated by distance
with the sound of a tunneled whistle these things are taken

and you feel something less than the wind leaving even
as you move toward it. Love and mourning march out
of the little holes in your skin. *Are we there yet,* the little ants ask.

Someone you may or may not know is singing. As you listen
the stream precipitates in the fjords of your eyes.
So you are taken, instant by instant
by what is taken from you.

IMMUNIZATION

You want to be dark.
You cannot.
You are pale.
Blue white knuckles and chicken bone fists.
Big teeth made of glass
rot through.

Wake up, the cavity has risen.
Let there be light.
Sleeping seam in the belly—
only one stitch left to cut—and everything spills out. Stars spill out.
It turns out you are burning.

*

What does not spill
spills eventually. I wake to slip
somewhere close to the bottom of it,
wake up tearing from many parts of the body bag,
fumes erupt from a bud in soft coral.

Constantly leaking.
I can teach you.
Put a little bit of the juice inside some tissue,
tuck it in a small blue box, tuck it in a pocket.
Feel it all day, like a new organ.

*

Dawn is a slot machine.
Out rushes golden coins in golden tresses.
Dawn awakening along
the thickened down of human form.
A voice tacks post-its to my eyes, to my ears.

Will I die alone?
I see tentacles,
little budding babies inside each round suckhole.

Dawn reminds me. Dawn is mindful like rabies.
You've been given milk mounds.
You've been given udder wisdom.

I pluck out the seeds.
I fry the eggs.

*

Morning.
Pull the handle anyway.
Money smells of mixed skins and alloyed metal
a pile of iron on my chest.

I've slipped on some kind
of purchased snow, fallen into myself.
I like it.
Deep tissue injection.
The needle is long and strong. Like a dash.
All my mothers like it too.

THE LIVING

The trees outside St. Mary's are queued up like dried arteries
though it is the heart of March.
Black ice on the ground.
The Midwest has the sort of personality
that makes me worship cold blank plains
like the face of someone I want love from, basic needs
tied up in a cloth sack, everything in it hard and dry
and clean. Cleanliness is mistaken for liveliness. Relief
for affection. How do I get from here to there?
What can I eat there? Will someone be there?
My true face is that of a potato. I have many eyes, but see nothing.
I'm afraid of the dark and bury myself in my fears.
That is what the spring invites. The first cardinal today
filled up the net of branches by the house. Yes, its small body
filled up the whole net. The changing temperature makes me porous.
Something else that is small and black perches on an ice block and caw
caw caws. Cardinals leak from the body.
I am afraid too much sight can kill me.
There is no such thing as inner space.
I am completely full. Maybe there are a few pockets between my kidneys
or the lobes in my upper midsection but it's tight. Too much seeing
would rip something. It happens all the time. Soon I think
I must deflate. I won't get there in time.
Why does everything look the same? Am I looking at a map
or a tree, or the hand of a dying man? Don't go. Don't go.
I drink with my eyes. When I try
to explain anything, some part of something, somebody dies.

DUCK DUCK GOOSE

I purchase a book on violence. The guns in the glossy pages line up
in a pretty garden spree, deep with chambers.

It is actually a book about the body.
The moral is Open the Body like the Goose's, the one filled with golden eggs.

I hear the cracking of the blue shell of dawn
as I look from page to leaf to page. Thin like skins.

Nothing comes out of the paper. I sit and take shots and wait
and take more shots. Is it still a game if you're the only player?

This is actually a book about alchemy.
Lead hitting gold. Nests of metal bees.

I want to be alone just long enough
to feel the trigger of longing and the mistake of it.

This is its bookmark. We are one third asleep
at all times, guarding our chapter of amnion and wind.

Inner nudity turns into static.
Each riddle is a bullet. Each journey a ring around a mental pivot.

Each targeting our one ever-bleeding legend
wrapped up in all sorts of literal objects.

Something gold falls out of the hatched body.

QUEST

I filled the bad
wolf with stones
I filled the bad
wolf with babies
the wolf in the pack
the wolf in your clothes
white wolves
in the tree
white goats
on the ground
the wolves of your skin
the goats of your hair
colony of wolves inside you
red wolves wolves of blood
blue black wolves the shape of stones
how many do I have to shoot
with my hollow bullets
howls in the tree
not leaves

*

You said

The beet root is truth
and it grows
toward us
and us is in the nickel

of the earth
blind red
with no body
with no sweetness
bulged midrib
what you don't know
is that I am
not a line
not a root
with eyes
but I am the eyes
all the eyes
all the tails
of the beet root
and you are blind to me
and I fill you
with eyes

*

Your allergies were so severe
you could not breathe
through your nose.
Your sighs
filled my ears. Wet beige sighs.
My ears were shells.
Your sighs were meat.
They ate sand.
Pearls plugged the canal

*

You are the
wolf now
the wolf a howl
howl a color
only I can see
I am made of howls
they nest in me
I am the silence
between howls
in the snow
rabbit pawed
howls divide
you close

*

What is that is that blood in the snow on the
ground no
that is plant juice root juice
boiled beet juice
from the wolves foray into the soup
how like us the bulbed stuff is
like our cunts

*

I said the potatoes would speak.
Live together in a plot of land.
How great, you thought.
It would be great for gathering tomptes.
There are wolves in this picture.
My plot is wolves

*

Tell me when I should stop

*

Stop now.

You said stop now.

I'm not worried.
I can live
without a pulse.

A howl does not need a body

*

Quiet.

Quiet.

PETS

Since I have known the plains, I have seen revelation.
Not mine, my brother's revelation—
a solid beat behind the sky, something bloated with blue light
staggering against evening's velvet curtain.
More terrible because it is not mine, and better, because
legendary spots should remain legendary.
I hope mine never arrives. No one should tell me
that my isosceles dream of knifing the other woman
is less urgent than the molten gold of his love.
Gold and knives are no longer relevant. Nor is the ravished brother
or the chosen one who saw the rabid squirrel of my true self.
Though it is true that a mad squirrel lives inside my trunk.
I am a mouth without an ear, wasting glamorously away in a cage.
My chinchilla mate is gone, the one who listened
to the spot behind the sky. The chinchilla believed that the sky
was a thing like frosted glass. Perhaps he will return.
I'm sorry things degenerate. I have a room for thoughts depraved.
I can't turn anything away. It's a farm in here.
Everything that waiting breeds.
Acorns upon acorns of poisonous raptures
fill up and stopper the faults in the doorway.
As for the other room, it is a room so bright
I cannot enter. I can't give it a name.

GROCERIES

List a.

Every list I write is meant to be the last one.
This is the last list I will ever write.

Whatever is in that list can be linked together like pieces of
a child's play set, a dinosaur bone, a human bone.

This is a list of excerpts from a potion that saturated my life
in a place I shall, (to cultivate a sense of distance), call *Fern City*.

It is the discovery of the drive to backtrack, to scuttle,
curl back into constant hypnosis and hook up with blackouts.

The list continues only if you read it.
It is moving right now, written by pressurized eyes.

Eyes are like rubber tires. They take you places.
Do a lot of traveling. I try not to puncture mine, but they leak.

My great fear has always been immediacy.
Being pulled from a vapor state into the bodyworld. This happens

when I cross Gorham and discover that I am crossing the spectrum
between daydream and road-kill. That is real.

Also when someone delicious and bud-like divined to me the reason
why the next few years of my life was going to be spent in hell

which is sometimes called Fern City, because flames are fern beautiful.
Because I am not beautiful, and neither was he.

It rains, the melting candle of the sky.
Somebody I don't know once said

that everything is like everything else.
As for my mind, it isn't anywhere,

though I suspect it is made up
of burr-shaped ideas that catch onto other people's clothing.

List b.

You are most like those you walk down the aisles in Wal-Mart with:
A horrifying discovery for some. Who did I spend my time with in Fern?

Fern City was shaped like a fish bone; that's why it's called Fern City.
Does that make sense?

Paths branched off at right angles from the beam of my enlightenment
and each one dropped off at a point, each one progressively shorter.

I always returned to the spine, the titles of things.
I always returned to the white matter, branching tenderly like wet fern.

One of the paths caught in my throat and I nearly died.
Now I only eat de-boned sardines.

The bones come out nicely, delicate as wings falling from trees.

In Fern City, I pushed a cart around, accumulated things.

List c.

The Mystic said: The longer your list of disquiet, the smaller your God.

God is quiet like the mouse. The mouse is actually a season, one that
makes me think of quivering firs.

My god is so small that I have swallowed him.
And that was how Eve got her Adam's apple.
That's one to cross off the list.
Next?

A can of sardines: I am a fisher of men. I have learned that to be a fisher of men
is to be a fishing net, which leaves grooves on my thighs
and does not fill up in the wind.

One tuna steak: Mayonnaise is an ingredient in tuna salad.

Man 2, whom we can call *n* as a variable,
raved about the tuna melts in that restaurant
by the capitol which lit up at night like a holiday.

n was allergic to salt water.

Syrup of Ipecac: Cooking for oneself can be fun.

There was no reason to stop eating after awhile, and it was fun
to eat for two in addition.

It became a game of pretend-pregnancy. *What is love*, you ask.

Lactaid: Most of the world is lactose intolerant.
I hear that women grow more tolerant when they lactate.

Sugar: and spice and everything nice.
What little girls are made of.

By which they mean fir and highly flammable pine needles. That's what
little girls are made of.

Cowpie cookies: Fat cows fail to jump over the moon.

Turpentine: Painting is therapy. Creative people may need a lot of therapy.
Vincent himself wisely noted, to know God is to love many things.
He needed a lot of therapy.

Deodorant: I loved many things
about n.

List d.

God was everywhere in Fern City. Browning declared him the perfect poet.
n smelled like baby powder and showered obsessively. God beamed upon him
with rays of golden light.

Leg of lamb: In lambda calculus, one cannot define a function which
includes itself.

Nepenthe: I don't know how this list became a theological query.
I only wanted to say that n fell in love with someone else shortly before killing me
because I was too much of a dreamer.

She has a face like Angelina. Big lips like a marine creature.

Set of kitchen knives: I dreamed of n when I was with him. Like he didn't exist.
Too much with god, I was. The soul is a fatality.

n wanted to be a real number.

Now I've said it. Smite me now.

Seven deadly sins: *I will make you as helpless as a blind man searching for a path.*

Godiva chocolates: clumps of my passion filled the air like ribbons of gauze
around his stomach, sweet and milky and divided by a fishbone of hair.

Cocoa powder: when I cut him, milk flowed out, slightly cantaloupe in flavor.
Loneliness in the dark sense is a recent phenomenon.

Its particles suspended by the buoyancy of human dairy in a jug.

The economy of Fern City flourished with the light of thousands.

I like to look at city lights for that reason. Cubes of it arranged in a shelf of dark.

I practice flexing the muscle of unthought.
The young are terrified of losing themselves,
bitter and pure with recursive and Dionysian mourning.

List e.

Nobody in Fern City was good enough. The people looked and looked within themselves and then without themselves.

They began to hate each other.

Soap: Everyone was special, see.
Everyone secretly or blatantly desired to be celebrities in Fern City.

Nobody remembers their lines. Only TV stars remember the future.
Watching Fern City at night from the top of a hill is like watching TV.
Cubes of light.

A star relays a message from the past remembering the future. Kiss kiss, it says.
Static from the beginning of time sets up the finale.

But when Sisera fell asleep from exhaustion, Jael quietly crept up to him with a hammer and tent peg. Then she drove the tent peg through his temple and into the ground,

and so he died. When Barak came looking for Sisera, Jael went out to meet him. She said, "Come, and I will show you the man you are looking for."

Yes, yes, yes. Let the ancient speak for me.

I will leave your flesh on the mountains, and fill the valleys with your carcass.

How much do I love thee?

I will water the land with what flows from you, and the riverbeds shall be filled with your blood.

In Fern City I have seen god and what was the remedy. Many-eyed dragonfly, or a city lit up with electricity.

A universal Turing machine calculates its name
and the rattling cubes of hearts.

God is a girl in love. The martyring type.

Such suffering of Fern's citizens gives him purpose.

When I snuff you out I will cover the heavens, and all the stars will darken;

Silence, which is not additive,
can be filled with anything.

LUSUS NATURAE

1. is

There is no letting go,
not until the end.

Only the gradual layering of leaves upon leaves, the soggy
flaps of impressions and this is me again, hello, craning my neck
against the high, blank brow of night.

How many times can night be described
without throwing it away?
I want to do more than throw.

Nothing goes away, says the boundless larynx
sending waves of peristalsis over the stage. That is night.

Purse of pelvic bone jangling
with something collapsible
and quiet with groundwater. That is night.

2. the trap

This is the knowledge that
over the mouthshaped drop in the ground
stretches only a thin linen.

Layer of thin insect's thread
woven into a delicate verge.
Something with lonely hands takes care of it,
fabricates a meticulous needlework.

We are threaded gently.
The eye is small
but we are smaller.

Crystals of breath
from the lungs of my kin, whose wings are thin,
whose eyes are shingled with hundreds
maybe thousands of pieces of each other.

Iridescent as money and
unrecognizable as sand.

Not only this
but even the wrung out stalks of the trees on the other side
of the pane warns me of insects
but not in the way you think.
The warning is directed at me.

I don't have six legs but I do have antennae,
I protest weakly.
Then I look in the glass and a lightbulb is crushed.

My eyes are legs walking over the cell of my room
made of dead trees
and the detritus of millennia-deceased.

3. fold

Only in our eyes exists miscreation.
This is why we have been granted darkness.
A small mental key

climbs up the tunnels in my head.
I hold the shining cochlea of night in my hand. Deaf and dumb
and dangling with whiskers.

I call and call into it,
and hold it to my ear like a dead sea-thing
and call into it with hearing.

Dawn closes. Flesh
remembers everything.
I don't know all of it.

But it's there, knocking around my pinched abdomen,
fluid coated currency.

What is listening?
Who's out there humming
beyond my white spacesuit?

The night is muscular and veined
like a husband.
I step into it.
I am married to it.

[GRENDEL IS A WOMAN]

1. NATIVITY, A NURSERY RHYME

Grendel is really a woman. He and his mother are one entity.

It was sometime in the 1700s, a great fire, when it stopped being true.

The story was so powerful it burst into flame, a wedding shower
of blueyellow blades. Browned to gold like a warm egg.

The excitement precipitated.

A pool of testosterone
and flakes of ash at the end.

To quench the fire, they drained the blood of a thousand scribes.
The egg was scrambled and the chicken blamed.

He had originated from the sea. Having no mother, sprout
from the inside of an eel-cave, peeled from living rock.

Part fish. Born whole, a woman.
A Darwinian marvel.

2. HUNGER

At first, he was pale and nude. You could see his gills, pink, intensely raw.
You would suspect that touching it would send him into spasms. You would be

touching something not-allowed. Your touch would singe, his flesh would curl.
By the age of two, the hair from his head covered his whole body.

The mammal side of him was full of fear. He had breasts. He was adopted
by the people of the sea, because he had a fish's tail. Very pretty, iridescent

and sometimes blue, sometimes green. Nice hips, the triangle of fur tapered
from perfection into a spread of hard scales. Grendel, they called him.

Grendel had a lovely singing voice, perhaps
better than all of them. They sang together in a great underwater cave

and their voices ripped through the waves. Whatever the songs touched
would tremble as if impaled. The songs became tables

upon which empty platters sat gleaming, and they loved the sight.
But Grendel was hungry. He was hungrier than all the rest. His hunger

made his body magnetic with the rhetoric of hollowness:
Little tiny spikes, little tiny scrapes, rippling with tiny implosions.

3. SONG

Sounds caught in the saltiness of their dim world
where separation was no concept.
They were a single, watery mass.
The whalefall that flaked from an invisible
ceiling were their thoughts. Pulverized bits of flesh
and the delicious crunch of cartilage and bone.

Grendel had a big mouth. He was made fun of
even though the inside of his mouth was pretty, and he knew it,
save the teeth
which looked like the inside of a shark, laid out in rows.

Grendel sang about metaphysics.
Everything was made of water. And his voice
grew sweeter, and higher, with the texture of unharvested pearl.

The people there feasted on krill and crustaceans.
They were undisturbed
in their landscape of echoes, untouched by true sunlight.

That was a long time ago.

Even so, he remembers the hunger. The hunger
stretched so far back
it pierced the eardrum of the fetal universe.

4. BEING BORN AGAIN FELT LIKE DYING

Grendel was half alive, spent most of his time asleep in a blank.
When he was awake, hunger threatened to pluck out the spicules
that held his watery fur together.
No such thing as crying down there.
His siblings sang, drunk on siblinghood, bathed in tears.
They flipped their silver bodies and the ocean jingled with the treasure
of their hard flat tones.

It was no accident, how Grendel found himself on a white shore. It was not
a reward, though it was his birthday. Feeling weird because of his body
which was full and curvaceous as the moon.

He remembered the first day again. The only other time this would happen
was thousands of years later in a university dorm, on salvia.

He'd done nothing to achieve immortality. In some ways, he resented it.

He was only a woman. Nobody knew what that was.
His tears mingled with seawater
and confused the lines of his body.

Incredible hunger. Hunger
that stretched each ribbon in the seams. Hunger for anything
not water, not the darkness of oysters, not the grotesque armory of lobsters
and frilled sea slugs.

Down there in the bliss, when someone was cut
with a rock, the stuff that flowed teased black.

Colorless hunger,
hunger that knew
another shade of black,
the layers of black
knowing that inside
the black was red.

Then it was time for him to rise
and break through the shimmering membrane.

The surface was solid. It was the splitting of something huge
inside of him. To see the horizon was to forget everything before that line

when the tendons of his green fuse stretched out to the vanishing point
and never bounced back.

His siblings said: (Don't forget us.)
But they looked and did not see him. They had always resented his voice.

Blind, unhindered of beauty, they had been safe
until he opened his mouth.

Grendel forgot them instantly. Air, for the first time,
entered and seared lungs he did not know he had.

There was a great heaviness where his skin met blank space.

He came to an understanding, wordless and without memory,
that this was disunity. Heaven and earth were formed
out of the salty chaos. Hell was there too, he would learn, knotty,
interesting, and much older than the other hemispheres.

5.

Then,
a ship
with sails like hymens
interrupted
the tightrope of dawn.

( )

Grendel yawned.
Air plugged his swallow hole.

(The mouth is a socket. The plug
a funnel.)

Grendel did not know what the clawing inside of him was, not even after he saw what he desired most. A crystal formed inside his body of water.

It must have been a prince, how it shone
and amplified the light.

Back then, everything was still water. Everything was water and desire the sucking of it down an invisible drain,

laughter the little bubbles in the blood with the rising body, quickly forgotten as Grendel slowly left the world of song and darkness, and touched himself.

He cleaved his body, every stroke. This must be
what it is like to be born, he thought, skin raw with himself.

This is the place where the hunters gather,
the beauty hunters,
the cruel ones,
the ones who do not have mothers.

6. MEMORY WILL BECOME A HABIT

There had been turtles.
His hair stuck out everywhere as it dried in the sharp atmosphere
of incredible lightness.

Bodies on the ship
in the distance moved upright on wobbling sticks.

( )

Grendel touched himself where his legs would begin.
Tears germed, and a strange
mealy sensation, as if something crystallized. It filled him with joy.

He perched on the bluegray back of the large turtle, scales flaking off,
browned like old leaves, old leaves being something new. He called to the
shadows on the ship, crushed out a long whistling hymn, crushed the sensation
of remembering a history no one experienced.

He held himself up and spread his rings, gargoyle-shaped, the crush streaming
from his big mouth thick as minced meat.

Nobody had heard such crying before.
Grendel's voice slammed pockets of space inside the sailor's watery chests.

But this is only one version of the memory...

( )

Grendel himself, prompted by a pimple-faced journalist, attempted to retell the encounter with the ship or the shipwreck but could not confirm whether or not he was singing.

There were human ears
plugged with wax,

certainly, but the only other surety, he said, was the conviction that death was close should the unknown hero pass right through his consciousness
with those unhearing airs, with that distracted gaze...

The mystic who saw across time, they dragged unshaven to the court.
Once again, they were to convict Grendel of first-degree murder. The mystic scoffed and fluttered like a flatfish. He had a way of melding into the background.

The mystic opened his dark mouth: (If he had been conscious he would have been annihilated at that moment!

All that had happened was that Ulysses had escaped.
All that he wanted was to hold as long as they could to the radiance that fell from Ulysses' great eyes.)

(But there were other men who died!) cried the court.

The mystic whirled around in his seat. (The inconceivable happens.) he declared.
Dark creatures slithered from his throat, lifted their blind, tiny heads to the light.

It was possible. That Grendel perched upon the back of a great turtle
and folded into his core ache
which could only exit through silence. Later, during the worst days, the silence
of his huge morbidity killed as only a machine could kill,
in perfect distribution of pressure.

A young woman with a yellow notepad and a pinched face
opened her pink mouth (Grendel, what is it like to be immortal?)

(It's like death.) said Grendel.
Inwardly, he wondered
what would happen
if he were cut into fist-sized cubes. Would he feel? And if not,
what is it to neither live
nor die? How long is infinity felt? Would he hunger? Would the hunger
multiply with the number of slits or sides?

(That's all I am.) he said (Hunger.)

(Are you hungry?) The young woman asked, perking her little breasts.

Of all eyes on him, only the mystic's were sympathetic, like a dog's.
The mystic's eyes were directed to the far wall behind him. Grendel felt that
they were alike.
(There is infinite hope.)
the dogman said.
(But not for us.)

7. GRENDEL'S FUR FELL OUT AND AGAIN
HE WAS PALE AND NUDE

Before the fixation with land and the one hero which populated it,
Grendel's life was a continual waterboard of discovery. Maybe it was puberty.
Hair and blood
and rubbery bones. Nothing fitting anywhere.

When the blood came leaking spirit, the people quarantined him.
(The sharks will sniff you out.) they said, rolling the huge stone door.
His nipples darkened to a black like newborn eyes. The newborn eyes looked out.

Grendel decided to forgive them. After all,
they had no concept of injury. What could they have done?

In the wet jet black he groped his way around the cave,
followed the gristly rustle of shadow through long tunnels.

There was someone else in there with him. She sat in a nest of human bone
and had a mouth with no lips,
and this liplessness opened further into the labyrinth.

(I know what you want.) said the sea witch.

8. THE BEST THING

The hunger nudged him with damp fleshy wings.
(I will do it.) said Grendel, and he became as pale as death.

(You have the sweetest voice of any who dwell here in the depths of the sea,

the best thing you possess for the price of my draught. My own blood
must be mixed with it, that it may be I am your mother, when once you had none.)

The sea witch took a pair of horrible scissors
and carpeted her lair
with the flush of Grendel's castration.

Grendel was a woman, but the witch in the underwater night had mistaken
something he did not know he had
for something he did not know he could lose.

She put the tongue in a jar.
Grendel was crying.

Out of him the tangled bellowing of a land creature.

As a parting gift, the witch gave him a handbook
decorated with exoskeletons. (I made it myself.)
She tried to sound tender (You will make tears without water.
That will be time
falling from you.

Secure yourself before you run dry.)

That was how he came into the possession of a great secret.
A few thousand lipless years
encapsulated in an hourglass. Each year
a pinprick of sand
within rounded numbness.

9. THOSE WHO CANNOT CRY SUFFER MORE

The second time he breached the surface, it was still night.
Stars made him dizzy.

The little needles of white
and the combustion of air, everything flying apart from everything else.

He cried from every pore of his body. He felt his throat, bloated
with dead larynx, the new splatter of his body, the hollow in his head.

The negative between his new legs, this rang through eardrum skin.
Grendel could only think
of the young sailor with large black eyes.

Around his body he wrapped his thick, oily hair. It was cold.
He began to thirst. The sky throbbed. Grendel thirsted.

He slept in a small cave by the shore and thirsted.

One morning, there was a whale
beached on the far end of the island. It was large with vibrating.
Grendel reached out and touched the rubbery skin around its one exposed eye.
(I know you.) he said voicelessly.

Its whale eye stared, spiced with sand. (You cannot speak.) Grendel continued.
Two silences traveled and made interference waves. Little sparks
floated from the island.

Grendel wanted to save her, but in his heart a hunger

told him to keep her. In a way, he knew, that was rescue. (Come.) he mouthed.
His new legs
that hurt like walking on carnivorous stones
were powerful enough to carry the whale back into the alcove and into
the black lake and he named the whale
and called her Polyphemus.

(No one will know you're here.) Grendel meant to say.
The whale was exhausted and lay on her side in the shallow water. One eye
faced stone heaven.

10. POLY

Before he achieved immortality, loneliness was an illness like any other ill.
He and Polyphemus had their quiet, and they waited for it to pass
the way all things passed.

It is normal for loneliness to erupt in someone when the rebellion of early life
starts plastering propaganda for the edges of things
and the universe contracts in increasingly terrible pulses.

In many cases loneliness is a symptom of separation, which is a drug.
Life, he understood, was a psychedelic side effect.

Sometimes Polyphemus let Grendel walk inside her
and feel around the open spaces of internal consciousness, which was like
the other side of a mirror. Not different from the outside,
dripping with something foul smelling, limited by muscle and protein chains.
Except there was no blue sky.

The day Grendel rescued the sailor,
pale yellow light broke through the sky-pane
once the sea ceased its salted spasms.

The stone clock began for the first time to mean. It began to groan under
the weight of the sun, dragged the carriage across the dark red
of his new shadow.

11. IT

> What a beauty!
> What a man!
> How his beauty dangles and hangs!
> How he shines!
> How his body makes smooth lines!
> This is something
> Born to be worshipped.

(Who are you?) the sailor asked.
The stone cave was full of echoes, which he and his crew mistook
for malicious creatures. They named various objects and shadows
after their ghosts and goblins.

Grendel darted into the shadows. He was afraid of man's beauty and man's soul
which leaked from Ulysses' pores easy as sweat, pheromonal, punctuated.
Out of Ulysses' eyes shot darts that could quench a horse though the word
horse did not yet have a meaning.

It may not have been Ulysses. There were many sailors, many men.

12. "2 SEXY CLOWNS: *IDENTICAL AND IDENTITY!*

Watch them in the famous mirror acrobat act!"

Beowulf found Grendel by accident. It was at a show, a circus performance, and one of the last of its kind. They met through a striation of metal bars being played by yellow lights.

The bars rung between them like struck keys.
Here was "Darwin's Daughter," whom some believed a saint. The second
virgin birth because of the perfect topography of his scar-free belly. Woman who
was not a woman, radical in the nude, grand as a Christmas tree with iron lights.

Beowulf was one of the crowd. To Grendel he stood out like an incision.
Neither believed
in fate, but fate believed in them.

Beowulf walked like a man. Around his regal torso
orbited two satellites, cherub children with crowns of yellow butter.

He had some white hairs around his temples and the eyes of a poet, heavy lidded,
and the cheekbones of a teenage girl with influenza.

Maybe through the shell-like growths over Grendel's arm and body Beowulf saw
his deceased wife, who had been the most beautiful woman in the world.

Beowulf pressed on the bars
through ivory silence. His children cried and cried and turned
their faces in like bashful ferns.

(That's not a monster.) lectured the good father. (That's a *woman* who is
very very sick. That's why she has all those warts. She's definitely not a tree.)

Grendel's thick kelp of hair was his only modesty.

In the next stall, a pile of straw and a hunger artist.
Grendel and the sack of bones shared a single sign.

People often complained of confusion. Who was the hunger artist and who was
the virgin? Were they both? Eventually Virgin was crossed out and replaced with
The Real Daphne.

13. ART'S SAKE

The artist's ribs jutted like feathers. Ruffled by straw and dirt, which the people called *Peoples' Flour* or *City Flour*. Which the artist claimed he would turn into cake.

(Nobody thinks about what it means to eat!) he cried with his withering orifice.

One day, the artist turned to Grendel: (I know what you're after. But I am the only one with the secret. Nobody survives this, but I will. This is the profession of life itself! Few get it. You, you'll probably get nothing but the spasms and agony of too much consciousness. Everyone knows, but nobody believes. You're all imitators! Imitators! All of you!)

(Call me the Great Poet!) cried the artist.

Nobody paid heed to the artist. Cage keepers beat him when he rattled the bars. But this did not last long and the artist was mostly forgotten.

Beowulf came to the cages every day the circus was there.

Sometimes Grendel gestured at the neighboring cage as a reminder to the keepers. *Feed the artist.* This happened when Beowulf was there. Beowulf liked that Grendel seemed a mystic. (Who are you pointing to?) he asked, not expecting an answer.

Beowulf was a doctor. He announced on the last day of the circus that he would save the tree-woman, and Grendel was abruptly inserted into the next chapter.

14. BY THEN HE'D STOPPED CHECKING THE HOURGLASS

But it was not for immortality that Grendel hungered.
In fact it was precisely the opposite. Grendel wanted to die,
and to die significantly.

When his skin erupted with strange barklike scales and lesions, he was relieved.
A smile spread tectonically across his pretty face as the hunger became bearable.

They used to lean against each other, back-to-back, bone xylophoning
the iron bars, grand as dumb elephants.

(We'll put up a play!) cried the artist,
(We'll change the audience's lives by inspiring them, setting an example of dying
that will teach them something about living...)
(But it is I who hunger.) Grendel mouthed, though his lips were unreadable.
Scabs crystallized over his pearly teeth.

15. THROUGH FINGERS OF NOTHING

It seemed to Grendel that people hung onto secrets without knowing
that it was only the hanging they wanted, and not the secret.

When he realized that he could move mountains, that it depended on
the edema in his heart,
that the same building could be haunted
one day and not the next
due to the temperature of his skin, suddenly
the ocean froze. Identical took on a new outfit. Identity stripped for a living.

This had never happened before. It was impossible. The ocean.
Literal oyster, the world was cracked open.

Even so, the cracking of a great secret simply worsened the widening dilation.
Spinning metal blades ground up inside him
an everlasting everlasting.

All the sidewalks in the world split into segregated squares
and in between the squares spontaneous cracks
like the cracked-shaped veins of prostrate private parts. Grendel saw that his life
was a puzzle. Walking across the long railroad of hot ember knives, each step over
a crack in the sidewalk created two new cracks. He could only walk over cracks.

He was so hungry. He tried to eat everything.
If he ate everything then nothing would be left to hunger for.
It would have to stop. At least that was the idea.
It was three thousand years old.

Tried to scream at the labcoats

(Did it ever occur to you that maybe I WANT to be drowned in my own fat?)

(But you will die. You have no intestinal tract.) they said.

Grendel ate, and vomited into a red bucket.

(Lady, what pleasure do you derive from regurgitation?) not expecting reply.

(My body isn't big enough–it is too big.)

He wanted the world to pass through him. All else unreal.

(Extreme case of compulsive eating.) they wrote.

(Complications: Ms. Grendel has a congenital deformity. Lack of excretory system. Ambiguous sex and oddly shaped pelvis. Lack of birth-scar.)

16. DO YOU BELIEVE IN

Sometimes the inexplicable effluvium of Beowulf's child-weathered hands.
Grendel didn't believe in love after he discovered it, but seeing Beowulf,

this old incongruity appeared. Realization of what began as a feeling. Internity
vacillating between the light and the silver plate a deep root had been pulled

out of red soil he felt the ribbed inner space pop. Beowulf glowed like a checker
that must be eaten, skipped, palmed, enveloped. It was not possible not to act.

Grendel would be turned inside out. Hunger became the shapes
emptiness could take. Beowulf was hot molten copper and Grendel the cast.

Through the solid muck he saw what he was to become. Through the skull the
aborted negative space.

Love is a hernia. The handbook said. No, maybe not. Most of it had been blurred
by spilt sea water maybe, love is a hermit. A hermit crab. A hearing. A herring.

Anyway, sometimes the inexplicable impression of Beowulf's soft hands
made eternity bearable. The quaking hunger flattened so slightly.

( )

Grendel stayed at the hospital for nine months. For the first five, both Beowulf and Grendel donned masks. Because their correspondence could not evolve fast enough, the nature of this barrier became a reef of significance. They played with each other and the pretence of heroism. He said it was like scuba diving, and Grendel was a majestic sea creature on the endangered species list. They passed a notebook back and forth, writing with colored pen. (Are you expecting me to grant you three wishes?) (Of course. You are a magic fish, after all.)

Most of the time, Beowulf responded by voicebox and Grendel wrote back in delicate hand with his delicate hand, nails marinated by one of the young nurses an eggplanty shade of purple. A hero is the complement of a hymen, and assumes the purpose to rip through veil after veil. The first layer was the tent, and then the perforated cage. The skin condition was more complicated, but not undoable.

Dr. Beowulf spent all the time by Grendel's bed.
Grendel molted like a great tree by scales and scales, and finally the octave
extracted the truffle of golden health; Dr. Beowulf saved the day.
Day was no longer such a dreadful word.
The distantly familiar tunnel-vision pulled Grendel to keeping time again.

(What are your wishes?)
(A kiss.)
(Through the gauze?)

The children came to visit Grendel once. The scars
were a smattering of stars on his lightening skin. Like two suns they rose
over the starch of the hospital bed. Their children's voices frightened
Grendel like dawn.
On each child's head, a god's hand.
(Emma, Nathanial, say hello to Grendel.)
(Hi Mam.) said the girl.
(Hi Missus Gretel.) said the boy, who was older and had a better voice.
They padded the woody silence of the room. Grendel could see the
unraveling of ectoplasmic chorus, which leaked from their tiny larynxes.

17. HE AND HIS MOTHER

It did not occur to Grendel that the children had a mother until much later. By this time he had regained much of his old vitality. They lived together well despite the children who buzzed around them like volatile gas molecules. Beowulf said that Grendel added heat to his life. He was dramatic for a doctor, and in the nights, which were chaste, he dispelled indigo words poxed with stars. (You are my little starfish.) (You have the most beautiful eyes I have ever seen.) In the dark, Beowulf could not read what Grendel wrote in the notepad. It was pure, like the inside of an appendix. Each minute between had the same historical scope as the hand of a child in amber.

Yes yes! thought Grendel. Let me drown in the bitter brown blood of him. As if the room had become pregnant.

18. AND

Grendel grew restless and violent. They slept in separate beds because of his snoring. Nevertheless, Beowulf was grateful for the way Grendel kept the kitchen clean and the children occupied.

Beowulf eventually took a mistress, then several, though he loved Grendel as much as a man could love a speechless being. Sometimes Grendel hid inside the mansion walls, passing between the bricks and insulation, picking at the brittle wallpaper, eating termites and sharing food with friendly mice.

There is no better example of the separation between wisdom and age. How much has gone by and Grendel is only wise enough not to give in to wisdom.

With a great poker the flames were stoked, and his terror flickered to life.

19. WAIL

How did he end up in cave?
How many caves did he live in?

(Something in my heart pittering pattering
battering out.)
(Don't die! Don't die!)

Love is fear. No.
Two abstracts make one concrete.

The fear that solidified inside Grendel was knobby and jointed. It fit awkwardly
inside his swollen pericardium. The trees around the cave turned white.

So many ages later it is hard to even remember the name of the sailor.

It may not have been Ulysses who made Grendel immortal. Though the one year of his island stay left strange marks all over his body, marks of passion and of time filled with it.

Of course Grendel found that passion could mean anything.
It referred to almost everything
that happened. Passion referred to the way sand kicked
around his new, delicate feet.
Passion was Ulysses' third nipple.

Passion was the princess who was having a day at the beach when Grendel pulled the sailor from the water. The city on the island was filled with a kind people who called themselves the people of Aeaea.

Grendel's beautiful beautiful body felt a massive echo.

So the happening goes that after the princess stoked Ulysses back to life
from sea-death, Grendel took him
as the princess and her servants scrambled for help
and kept the hero in his stone cave and that was how
Polyphemus was killed.

Polyphemus was in the cave.
Polyphemus was lying in the black lake.
Polyphemus was too big for the black lake.

Polyphemus the whale was in the black lake where she was saved
when the hero was saved.

Because Ulysses gazed upon the whale and he saw a beast pleading for
the mercy of death. (Poly Poly Poly!) Grendel bloomed and discovered
that he no longer had tear ducts.

Sounds of warm water.

The echo of his nude female body ached for the salt of the sea. The burning stake
that was stabbed through Poly's one rolling eye made the cave smell
like grilled meat.

20. IRIDESCENT FEATHERS

It is true that Grendel only has one arm.
In modern times the handicapped are well accommodated.

When his arm was lobbed off it was as if the missing part served only to magnify
the defining drive of his life. Hunger reduced to a thickness
from which there was
no possible escape. The phantom became itself.

Sometimes his pet parrot lends him forgetfulness. But it was a doomed endeavor
from the start, because Grendel named the bird after the late Polyphemus.

Whenever Poly asks for a cracker, Grendel remembers.

But they share moments of stillness
and in these, Grendel is able to feel vaguely new again,
a feeling that grows more rare, and more rare, and more
with no perceivable limit.

Grendel has learned sign language. He likes to pretend he hasn't.

People are always curious. They try to distill the secret of immortality from him
and more than once he's almost died in experimental captivity.

He has learned the art of escape.

21. ASPIRATION

One of his most vivid memories: a dead dragonfly on the pavement

Grendel ambled past thinking (O dragonfly!) of god's miracles,
stopped and turned around. With his one arm he stooped toward the miracle.

A long time reaching it. He was so high, the height of his female anatomy
now less supple in tone. Bones knocking against each other like starving birds,
un-oiled ligaments squeaking.

The space in his head like an airport with the planes in midlanding.

God's miracle was horribly light; nothing was in his hand at all.

Suddenly Grendel popped into a box in which he could not fathom the senses.

The miracle's disproportionately gigantic head fell back like a baby's,
rustling with leaf-talk.
Its husks of legs smoked with something like desert.

Grendel shuddered and cried out. The tiny dragon fell to the ground! Its wings
beat at the gravity of light! Dragonfly! Dragonfly!
A dust mote ignited by sun drifted before his unfocused eyes, landed on
the tiny fringe of hair on his lip.

22. GREAT POETRY

At the entrance to the farmer's market, a handsome suit solicited
signatures. *Whales going extinct.* (We have thousands of expiring Lorcas but
only one Lorca.) he said, holding a placard with subtitles.

(Orca whales are actually dolphins.) said a lanky passer-by. He had multiple
piercings and dark lip-liner.

This was decades after the conclusion of what Grendel considered
the great drama of his life.
Even then, the voice of Beowulf stuck to the base of his skull like wet tobacco
dreaming of cancer and plant matter.

One of his best-loved secrets was that Beowulf had a special meaning
for the word dragon
and many jokes to go along with it. Dragonfly dragonfly dragonfly.

Each deep love had resulted in amputation.

Image of Beowulf playing with his pant zipper. (I strum my dragonfly dragon
fly dragon fly!)
(The miracle mosquito!)

Since the beginning Grendel thought the male privates a solemn amateur
who cannot walk because of the weight of its massive, grainy wings
all folded into blankets of raw skin.

In such a world, dragons, which are derivatives of fish, do not breathe fire,
but are prone to exaggerations of their own waterlogged powers.

23. NO EXIT

Once in a while Grendel
returns to the beach
where he can gaze
vaguely at his birthplace.

Now he cannot remember
what had inspired him
to surface in the first place.

The smell of ruin flows sweetly.

24. EPIGRAM

Then my face won't be there
to be covered in death...

—Beowulf